T0389921

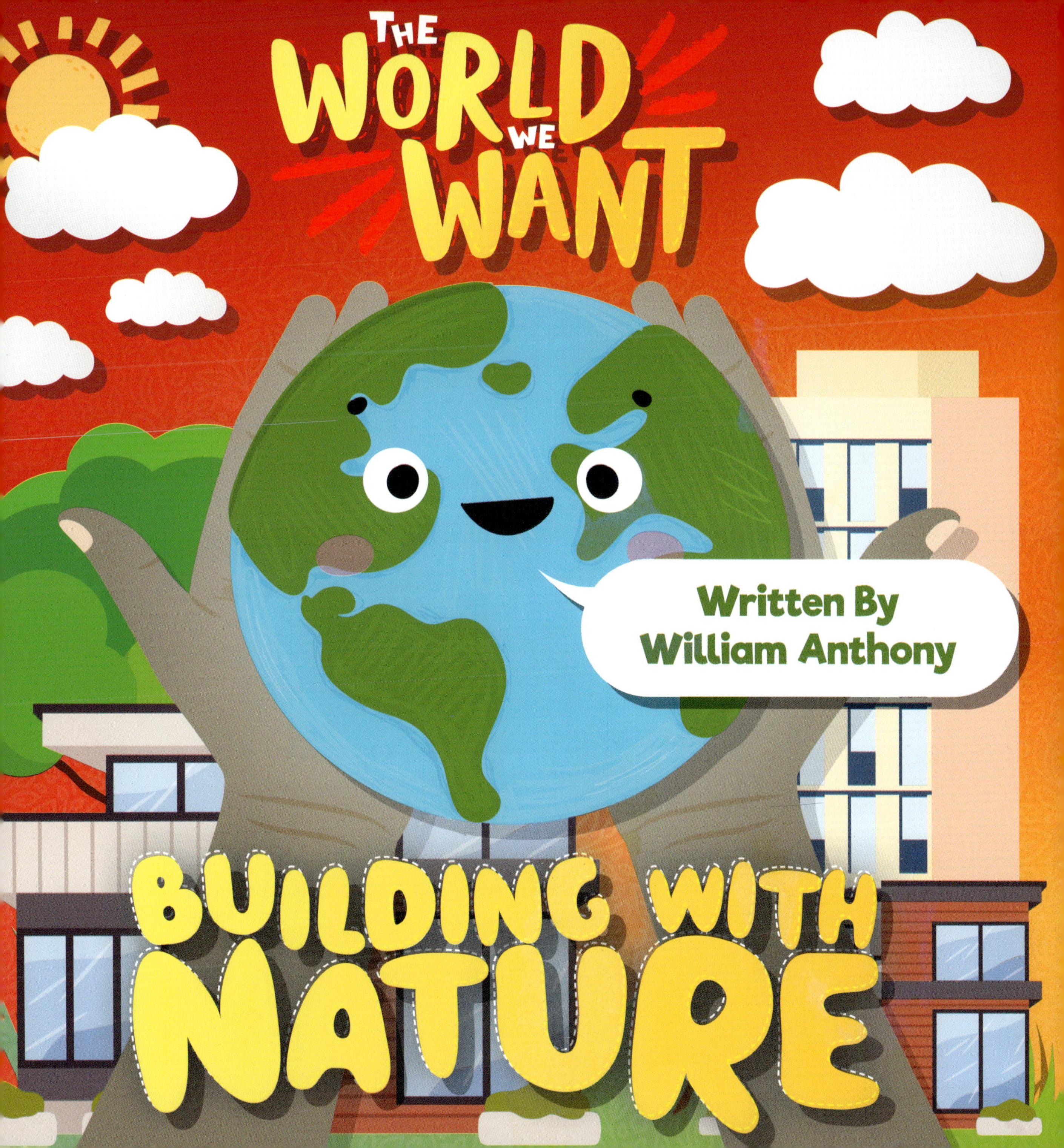
THE WORLD WE WANT
Written By
William Anthony
BUILDING WITH NATURE

Building with Nature © 2024 BookLife Publishing
This edition is published by arrangement with BookLife Publishing

sales@northstareditions.com
888-417-0195

Library of Congress Control Number:
The Library of Congress Control Number is available on the Library of Congress website.

ISBN
979-8-89359-333-4 (library bound)
979-8-89359-417-1 (paperback)
979-8-89359-387-7 (epub)
979-8-89359-363-1 (hosted ebook)

Printed in the United States of America
Mankato, MN
092025

Written by:
William Anthony

Edited by:
Rebecca Phillips-Bartlett

Designed by:
Rob Delph

All facts, statistics, web addresses and URLs in this book were verified as valid and accurate at time of writing. No responsibility for any changes to external websites or references can be accepted by either the author or publisher.

PHOTO CREDITS

All images are courtesy of Shutterstock.com, unless otherwise specified. Front Cover – Tanarch, cosmaa, Hafid Firman, GoodStudio, venimo, StockSmartStart. 4&5 – ixpert, narikan. 6&7 – Artography, KK Art and Photography, kukurund, Peter Gudella. 8&9 – jgolby, Flystock. 10&11 – Pommy.Anyani, Irene Miller, Scott Biales DitchTheMap. 12&13 –Diana Taliun, CartoonGift, GoodStudio, FamVeld, CartoonGift, RimDream, xpixel, GeorgOTS, Oksana_Slepko. 14&15 – New Africa, ANGHI, ePromoters. 16&17 – ANGHI, ePromoters, Standret, wavebreakmedia, New Africa. 18&19 – Oleg1824, B Brown, thoughtsofjoyce. 20&21 – Jeanette Virginia Goh, Sarah2, kozirsky, Alexeysun. 22&23 – PhotopankPL, Luriya Chinwan, Dario Pena, Chadchai Krisadapong. Vectors throughout – Tanarch, cosmaa, Hafid Firman, GoodStudio, venimo, StockSmartStart.

CONTENTS

Words that look like this can be found in the glossary on page 24.

NO NEW PLANET

We all live on a planet called Earth. It is our home. We share our home with many animals and plants. They are all an important part of our planet's ecosystem.

YOU LIVE SOMEWHERE ON THIS PLANET! CAN YOU SPOT WHERE?

We need to look after the environment. This will help to keep our planet healthy. The best way to do this is to work together with nature.

BUILDINGS

You enter buildings every day. Your home is a building. Your school is a building, too. Buildings give us places to live, eat, work, and play. They might be built out of bricks, concrete, or even clay.

However, many buildings are created in ways that do not look after our planet. Forests are sometimes cut down to make space for buildings. This means some animals lose their homes.

The energy we use to power buildings can be harmful, too!

ECO-FRIENDLY BUILDING

It is important to build things in a way that does not harm the environment. This is called eco-friendly building.

Eco-friendly building is not just about making houses in a way that keeps Earth healthy. It is also about building houses that use fewer of our planet's resources over a long amount of time.

RAMMED EARTH

Making bricks can be bad for our planet. There is a way to avoid using bricks. People have used something called rammed earth to build houses for thousands of years.

RAMMED EARTH WALL

BRICK WALL

Rammed earth is dirt that has been pressed very tightly. This turns it into a material similar to rock. Building with rammed earth is much better for the environment than using bricks.

Clay is often used to make rammed earth. Let's make our own clay house!

1.

Ask an adult to help you find some air-dry clay. Pull it apart into two big lumps.

2.

Firmly flatten your first lump of clay, just like rammed earth!

3. Shape this lump of clay into walls.

4. Firmly flatten your next lump of clay.

5. Shape your clay into a roof.

6. Add the roof on top of the walls. Leave it to dry for two days.

7. Paint your clay house!

ECO-INSULATION

People need to stay warm in the coldest parts of the year. Many people heat their homes using energy. However, using lots of energy can harm our planet.

Some people use radiators to heat their homes. This uses lots of energy.

We can help the planet by insulating our homes well. Insulation helps keep a house warm. We can use natural materials such as cotton to insulate houses.

Let's build a super cozy fort using cotton!
1.
Gather some objects made of cotton. Bed sheets, pillowcases, and blankets are often made of cotton. You could try some of these!
If you are not sure, look for the word "cotton" on the label.

2\. Find a perfect space at home to make your fort.

3\. Use something big to create your roof, such as a bed sheet or blanket.

4\. Make it warm and cozy inside by using pillows or smaller blankets!

RECLAIMED WOOD

People often use wood when constructing new buildings. However, forests are usually cut down to make new wood. This is harmful to animals and to Earth's air.

One way to keep our planet healthy is to use reclaimed wood instead. This is old wood that is used again for a new job. It helps the planet!

Let's try making a model house using reclaimed wood!
You will need lots of old popsicle sticks. Save them every time you have an popsicle.
You will also need glue and paint.

Now it is time to experiment! Start gluing your sticks together to make your house. Think about these questions.

LOVE OUR PLANET

Do you have any new ideas for how to keep Earth healthy?

Our planet needs to be looked after. It is up to us to do it. People have come up with lots of interesting and smart ways to build with nature.

Whether it is with rammed earth houses, cotton insulation, or building with reclaimed wood, you can help create the world we all want.

GLOSSARY

CONSTRUCTING building or making something

ECOSYSTEM everything that lives together in an environment

ENERGY usable power that comes from heat, light, electricity, and other things

ENVIRONMENT the surroundings that an animal, plant, or human lives in

EXPERIMENT try different ideas to see what happens

MATERIAL something that is used to make other things

NATURAL not made by humans

NATURE the world around us and everything in it that is not made by humans

RESOURCES a supply of something that can be used when it is needed

INDEX